Sports Illustrated KIDS

HOCKEY STATS
AND THE STORIES BEHIND THEM

What Every Fan Needs to Know

by Shane Frederick

CAPSTONE PRESS
a capstone imprint

Sports Illustrated Stats & Stories are published by Capstone Press,
1710 Roe Crest Drive, North Mankato, Minnesota 56003.
www.mycapstone.com

Library of Congress Cataloging-in-Publication Data
Names: Frederick, Shane.
Title: Hockey stats and the stories behind them : what every fan needs to know / by
Shane Frederick.
Description: North Mankato, Minnesota : Capstone Press, 2016. | Series: Sports
Illustrated Kids. Sports Stats and Stories | Includes bibliographical references,
webography and index.
Identifiers: LCCN 2015039060| ISBN 9781491482179 (Library Binding) | ISBN
9781491485866 (Paperback) | ISBN 9781491485903 (eBook PDF)
Subjects: LCSH: Hockey—Statistics—Juvenile literature. | Hockey players—
Statistics—Juvenile literature. | Hockey—History—Juvenile literature.
Classification: LCC GV847.5 .F73 2016 | DDC 796.962--dc23 LC record available at
http://lccn.loc.gov/2015039060

Editorial Credits
Nick Healy, editor; Ted Williams, designer; Eric Gohl, media researcher;
Tori Abraham, production specialist

Photo Credits
Dreamstime: Jerry Coli, 12; Getty Images: Bruce Bennett Studios, 23, 28, 44 (top);
Newscom: Cal Sport Media/Joe Camporeale, 11, Icon SMI/Alan Schwartz, 39,
Icon SMI/Mark Goldman, 33, Icon Sportswire/Rich Graessle, 14, Icon Sportswire/
Steven Ryan, cover, 1; Sports Illustrated: Al Tielemans, 31, Bob Rosato, 17, Damian
Strohmeyer, 29, 32, David E. Klutho, 10, 13, 15, 20, 21, 27, 42, 43, 44 (bottom), Hy
Peskin, 18, John D. Hanlon, 25, 34, Robert Beck, 36, 38, 40, 41, Simon Bruty, 6–7, 8,
16, Tony Triolo, 5, 9, 45

Editor's Note: All statistics are through the 2014–15 NHL season unless otherwise
noted.

Printed in the United States of America.
904

STATS ON ICE

On December 19, 1917, the first night of play in the National Hockey League (NHL), the statistics started piling up.

Dave Ritchie of the Montreal Wanderers scored the first goal in league history, 1 minute into a game against the visiting Toronto Arenas. He later added another goal in the 10-9 victory. Meanwhile, in Canada's capital city of Ottawa, the Montreal Canadiens were getting the first of many superstar performances they'd see over the next century. Joe Malone scored five goals in a 7-4 victory over the hometown Senators.

Malone scored 44 goals in 20 games that season, and although assists wouldn't be officially tracked until the next season, he helped out on four other goals. His teammate, goaltender Georges Vezina, allowed 84 goals in 21 games for a 3.93 goals-against average.

Today we can look back at those early games and understand something about what happened because statistics were recorded and preserved. Statistics are the numbers that tell the story of games, seasons, eras, and careers. The game of hockey has changed over the years, but statistics allow us to compare players and contrast styles.

TABLE OF CONTENTS

As the NHL added games to its season, the numbers grew. The Canadiens' Howie Morenz became the first player to break the 50-point mark, doing so in 1928. The Boston Bruins' Phil Esposito burst through two ceilings—topping 100 points in 1969 and 150 two years later. Edmonton Oilers star Wayne Gretzky scored more than 200 points in 1981–82, becoming the first (and only) player to hit that milestone. He also topped Malone's longtime mark of 2.4 points per game.

Over time, more statistics have been introduced to better explain and analyze the sport, from plus-minus in the 1960s to the odd-sounding Corsi and Fenwick in the 2010s. Who are the players behind the numbers? How did they reach those marks? What do their stats mean? There are as many good stories in hockey as there are stats.

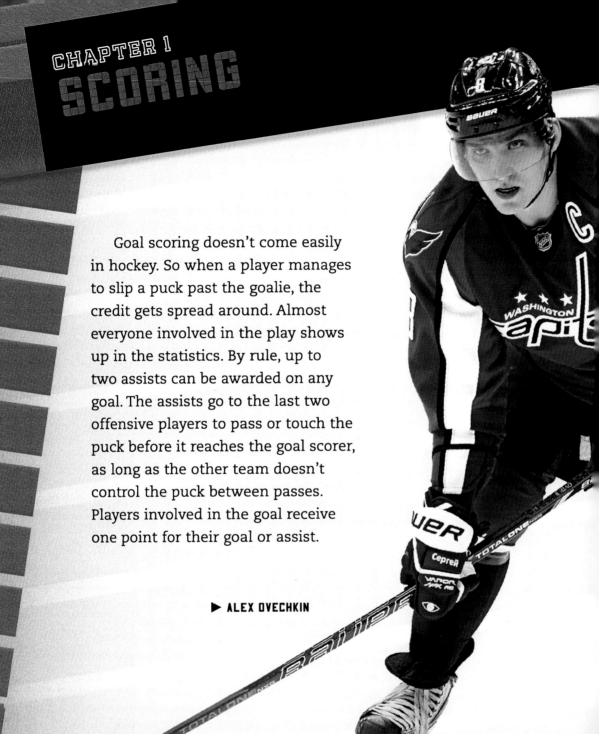

Goal scoring doesn't come easily in hockey. So when a player manages to slip a puck past the goalie, the credit gets spread around. Almost everyone involved in the play shows up in the statistics. By rule, up to two assists can be awarded on any goal. The assists go to the last two offensive players to pass or touch the puck before it reaches the goal scorer, as long as the other team doesn't control the puck between passes. Players involved in the goal receive one point for their goal or assist.

▶ ALEX OVECHKIN

Assists have been tracked in the NHL since the 1918–19 season, when Newsy Lalonde was credited with 10 assists and led the league with 32 points. In the speedy game of hockey, however, modern technology has made it easier to reward points, especially a secondary assist that took place further back in the play. Official scorers use video replay, including slow-motion, to decide which players should get credit for goals and assists.

The league's top point scorer isn't necessarily the player who scores the most goals. Rather, he is the one involved in the most goals. Of the NHL's top nine scorers in 2014–15, only the Washington Capitals' Alex Ovechkin had more goals (53) than assists (28). The Dallas Stars' Jamie Benn won the scoring title with 87 points (35 goals, 52 assists).

THE GREAT ONE AND THE KID

▲ SIDNEY CROSBY

During the 2013–14 season, Pittsburgh Penguins star center Sidney Crosby dominated the scoring charts. A superstar since he burst on the NHL scene at age 18, he led the league with 104 points. He scored 36 goals and assisted on 68 others to reach his total. He was the only player in the league to rack up more than 100 points that season. It was the fifth time in nine seasons Crosby had passed that milestone.

Thirty years earlier the Edmonton Oilers' Wayne Gretzky scored 205 points (in the 1983–84 season). It was one of four seasons in which The Great One, as Gretzky was known, finished with more than 200 points. In 1985–86, he dazzled Edmonton fans (and most other hockey fans throughout the world) by scoring 52 goals and dishing out a whopping 163 assists. That gave him 215 points. It's a single-season record that will likely never be broken.

Gretzky holds the NHL's career scoring record with 2,857 points. His total includes 894 goals and 1,963 assists, which are both records. Gretzky dished out so many assists—often from the space behind the opponent's net—that if you took away all of his goals, he'd still hold the points record. He'd have 76 more points than his former teammate Mark Messier.

MOST GOALS IN A SEASON

Rank	Player	Team	Goals	Season
1.	WAYNE GRETZKY	OILERS	92	1981–82
2.	WAYNE GRETZKY	OILERS	87	1983–84
3.	BRETT HULL	BLUES	86	1990–91
4.	MARIO LEMIEUX	PENGUINS	85	1988–89
5.	TEEMU SELANNE	JETS	76	1992–93
	PHIL ESPOSITO	BRUINS	76	1970–71
	ALEXANDER MOGILNY	SABRES	76	1992–93

▶ WAYNE GRETZKY

SECOND TO NONE

Are first assists more valuable than second assists? The NHL has started keeping better track of those numbers. In 2014–15, Vancouver Canucks winger Daniel Sedin led the NHL with 35 first assists, but he also had 21 second assists. Dallas Stars center Tyler Seguin had 33 first assists but just seven second assists. He also scored 37 goals, which ranked fifth in the league. New York Rangers defenseman Keith Yandle led the NHL with 30 second assists. He also racked up 16 first assists.

▲ DANIEL SEDIN

MOST ASSISTS IN A CAREER

Rank	Player	Assists
1.	WAYNE GRETZKY	1,963
2.	RON FRANCIS	1,249
3.	MARK MESSIER	1,193
4.	RAY BOURQUE	1,169
5.	PAUL COFFEY	1,135

A RARE FEAT

Wayne Gretzky holds 61 official NHL records, and many seem unlikely to be broken. In 2014, however, Colorado Avalanche rookie Nathan MacKinnon surpassed The Great One in one category. MacKinnon scored a point in 13 consecutive games. That was a record for an 18-year-old. But MacKinnon's run didn't come close to Gretzky's 51-game point-scoring streak. The record streak came at the outset of the 1983–84 season. Gretzky had 61 goals and 92 assists for 153 points during that stretch.

▶ NATHAN MACKINNON

11

▶ PHIL ESPOSITO

Most fans think of a game-winning goal as one involving some drama. Perhaps it comes as the result of an exciting play late in the third period of a tie game. Perhaps it ends an overtime game.

According to the statistic kept by the NHL, however, a game-winner is something simpler. It is merely the goal that gives the winning team one more than the opposing team's total. For example: In the case of a 4-1 victory, the game-winner would be the prevailing team's second goal, even if it came in the first period.

Not surprisingly, the most game-winning goals in history have come from some of the game's top goal scorers. Jaromir Jagr and Phil Esposito lead the all-time list. Curiously, Wayne Gretzky ranks just 15th with 91 game-winners.

MOST GAME-WINNING GOALS IN A CAREER

Rank	Player	Goals
1.	JAROMIR JAGR	129
2.	PHIL ESPOSITO	118
3.	BRETT HULL	110
	TEEMU SELANNE	110
5.	BRENDAN SHANAHAN	109

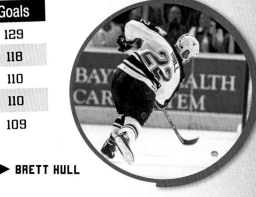

▶ BRETT HULL

In 2014–15 Alex Ovechkin, the NHL's top goal-scorer, also led the league with 11 game-winners. The New York Islanders' John Tavares scored the most overtime goals that season with four.

CLUTCH PLAYERS

The New Jersey Devils were skating in overtime. Jaromir Jagr received a pass in the neutral zone and rushed straight at the lone defenseman between him and the Ottawa Senators' goaltender. After a couple of dangles with the puck, Jagr ripped a wrist shot under the goalie's glove to win the game for the Devils. Not bad for an old man. At the age of 42, Jagr had scored his 19th career overtime goal, an NHL record. The next season, 2014–15, Jagr scored five game-winners (one in overtime) to lift his total to 129, another NHL record.

▶ JAROMIR JAGR

◄ JOE SAKIC

Tampa Bay Lightning sniper Steven Stamkos scored five overtime goals in 2011–12, a single-season record. He finished that season with 12 game-winners in all, four shy of the NHL record shared by Phil Esposito (who had 16 twice) and Michel Goulet. The Colorado Avalanche's Joe Sakic scored more playoff overtime winners than any player with eight.

CHAPTER 3

POWER PLAY PERCENTAGE

▶ ALEX OVECHKIN

A power play is awarded to a team when its opponent commits a penalty. The penalized player must sit in the penalty box for two minutes (or longer in the case of a major penalty) while his team skates with one less player than the other team. A power play's success is measured by calculating a percentage: goal-scoring power plays divided by total chances with the advantage. The NHL's best power-play teams usually score 20 to 25 percent of the time—or about one in every four or five power plays.

Alex Ovechkin is one of the most dangerous goal scorers in hockey. The powerful Capitals forward has led the NHL in goals five times, scoring 50 or more goals in six seasons. On the power play, he is lethal, blasting pucks past goalies from his favorite spot in the left circle. During the 2013–14 and 2014–15 seasons, nearly half of Ovechkin's goals were scored with his team on the power play.

MOST POWER PLAY GOALS, CAREER

Rank	Player	Goals
1.	DAVE ANDREYCHUK	274
2.	BRETT HULL	265
3.	TEEMU SELANNE	255
4.	PHIL ESPOSITO	249
5.	LUC ROBITAILLE	247

▲ DAVE ANDREYCHUK

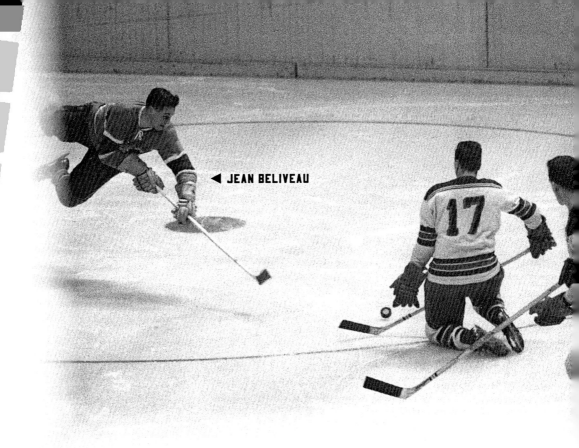

◀ JEAN BELIVEAU

GAME-CHANGERS

Teams feared penalties when they played the mighty Montreal Canadiens in the 1950s. Montreal's power play was so good that their beloved superstar and captain, Jean Beliveau, once netted a hat trick during the same minor penalty. He scored his three goals in a span of just 44 seconds.

Midway through the 1950s, the NHL decided to change its rules to slow down Montreal's potent power play. Instead of serving a full two minutes on a minor penalty, the penalized player was allowed to exit the box once a goal was scored. The change didn't seem to bother Montreal much. It was still the best team in the league, and it closed out the 1950s with five Stanley Cup championships in a row.

The Canadiens' success didn't stop there. The 1977–78 team, which was part of a four-year championship run, had a power play percentage of 31.88 percent. That's an all-time record.

The worst power play percentage for a season belonged to the 1997–98 Tampa Bay Lightning, who scored just 9.35 percent of the time. The team finished with the worst record in the NHL that season.

BEST POWER PLAYS, 2014-15 SEASON

Rank	Team	Power Play %
1.	WASHINGTON CAPITALS	25.32%*
2.	DETROIT RED WINGS	23.81%*
3.	PHILADELPHIA FLYERS	23.44%
4.	ST. LOUIS BLUES	22.31%*
5.	COLUMBUS BLUE JACKETS	21.72%

* made playoffs

CHAPTER 4

PENALTY KILL

When one team is working to score with an extra-player advantage, the other team is trying to prevent a goal. As with power plays, a penalty kill's success is measured by percentage: the number of successful kills divided by the total number of opponents' power plays.

The best penalty-killing team in NHL history was the 2011–12 New Jersey Devils, who had a success rate of 89.58 percent. They allowed just 27 power play goals in 82 games, while scoring 15 short-handed goals. They were helped by having one of the greatest goaltenders in hockey history, Martin Brodeur. That season the Devils advanced to the Stanley Cup Finals but fell to the Los Angeles Kings.

▲ MARTIN BRODEUR

BEST PENALTY KILLERS, 2014-15

Rank	Team	Penalty Kill %
1.	MINNESOTA WILD	86.32%*
2.	VANCOUVER CANUCKS	85.71%*
3.	PITTSBURGH PENGUINS	84.84%*
4.	CAROLINA HURRICANES	84.74%
5.	COLORADO AVALANCHE	84.65%

* made playoffs

▲ MINNESOTA WILD

The worst penalty kill in NHL history belonged to the 1979–80 Kings. They had a 67.7 percent success rate. Despite that poor performance, the Kings had a decent record. They were 30–36–14 that season, good enough to take second in their division and make the playoffs.

SCORING ON THE KILL

The Boston Bruins in 2010 netted three short-handed goals during the same penalty kill, scoring them in a span of 64 seconds.

CHAPTER 5
PENALTIES IN MINUTES

It's a simple fact: Penalties are part of hockey games. For individual players, penalties are measured by the number of minutes assigned to a particular infraction. Even if a goal is scored during a penalty, which ends the power play, a player is credited with a full penalty. Minor penalties are worth two minutes. Double-minor penalties are worth four minutes. Major penalties are five minutes. All misconducts, including game misconducts and match penalties (when a player gets kicked out of the game) go down as 10 minutes.

For a few players, a high total of penalty minutes is a badge of honor. Some people call such players enforcers; others call them goons. To these guys, time spent in the penalty box—or out of the game entirely—reflects grit and toughness. It shows their willingness to battle along the boards and to stand up for teammates. But penalties also mean putting teammates at a disadvantage, forcing them to play short-handed. That increases their opponent's chances to score, of course. It can also tire out a team's best defensive players, who end up playing extra minutes on the kill.

IN THE BOX

Chris "Knuckles" Nilan of the Boston Bruins was penalized 10 times for a total of 42 minutes in a single 1991 game. The total included six minors, two majors, a misconduct, and a game misconduct. In 1979 the Kings' Randy Holt received nine penalties for 67 minutes in one game.

COMMON HOCKEY PENALTIES

Penalties	Description
BOARDING:	HITTING AN OPPONENT FROM BEHIND INTO THE BOARDS
CROSS-CHECKING:	CHECKING A PLAYER WITH THE STICK, USING BOTH HANDS AND EXTENDING ONE'S ARMS
CHARGING:	SKATING SEVERAL STRIDES OR JUMPING TO CHECK AN OPPONENT
ELBOWING:	USING AN ELBOW TO HIT AN OPPONENT
HOLDING:	USING HANDS OR ARMS TO GRAB AN OPPONENT
INTERFERENCE:	HITTING OR IMPEDING AN OPPONENT WHO DOES NOT HAVE THE PUCK
ROUGHING:	SHOVING AN OPPONENT OR INVOLVEMENT IN A MINOR ALTERCATION
SLASHING:	USING THE STICK TO HIT AN OPPONENT
TRIPPING:	USING THE STICK OR PART OF ONE'S BODY TO KNOCK DOWN AN OPPONENT AT THE LEGS OR FEET

DIRTY OR DISCIPLINED?

The Philadelphia Flyers of the 1970s were known as the Broad Street Bullies. Their arena, The Spectrum, stood on Broad Street. And the team won with fighting and intimidation as important parts of its game plan. The Flyers won back-to-back Stanley Cup championships in that era. Their second title came in 1974–75, when winger Dave Schultz set a single-season record with 472 penalty minutes. By comparison, the most penalized player in 2014–15 was Pittsburgh Penguins winger Steve Downie, who had 238 penalty minutes. Since 1998–99 a player has reached 300 or more penalty minutes in a season just three times. That milestone was reached much more often in the 1970s and 1980s.

TIME WELL SPENT?

During a 2014 game between the Vancouver Canucks and the Los Angeles Kings, Canucks left wing Tom Sestito was credited with just one second of playing time. But that one second turned into nearly a half hour of penalties. Sestito got into a fight immediately after the puck dropped on his first and only shift, and the penalties piled up from there: five minutes for fighting, two minutes for instigating the fight, a 10-minute misconduct, and a game misconduct.

◄ DAVE SCHULTZ

The Broad Street Bullies put their opponents on the power play more than any other team. In the 1974–75 season, the Flyers allowed opponents 466 power plays. The next closest team allowed 326.

NHL teams don't play that way anymore. In 2014–15, the Chicago Blackhawks were the Stanley Cup champs. They were also one of the league's least-penalized teams, averaging 7.3 penalty minutes per game.

CHAPTER 6
GOALS-AGAINST AVERAGE

Scoring goals is important, but so is preventing them. A hockey team's last line of defense is the goaltender, the brave soul who guards the net against wicked slap shots, twisted wristers, and tricky tip-ins. Goals-against average (GAA) is the number of goals a goalie allows per 60 minutes—the length of a regulation game. A goalie can play more minutes in a game that goes to overtime. He can play fewer minutes in a game if he is replaced or leaves the net for an extra attacker. To find the goals-against average, divide the number of goals by the number of minutes played; then multiply that number by 60.

Goalie X gave up 16 goals in 358 minutes of ice time.

16 ÷ 358 = .045
.045 x 60 = 2.7

Goalie X has a GAA of 2.7.

Some critics believe GAA is not the best measure of how good a goaltender is. It measures only goals allowed. It doesn't measure the number of shots a goalie faces or how well the defense plays for him.

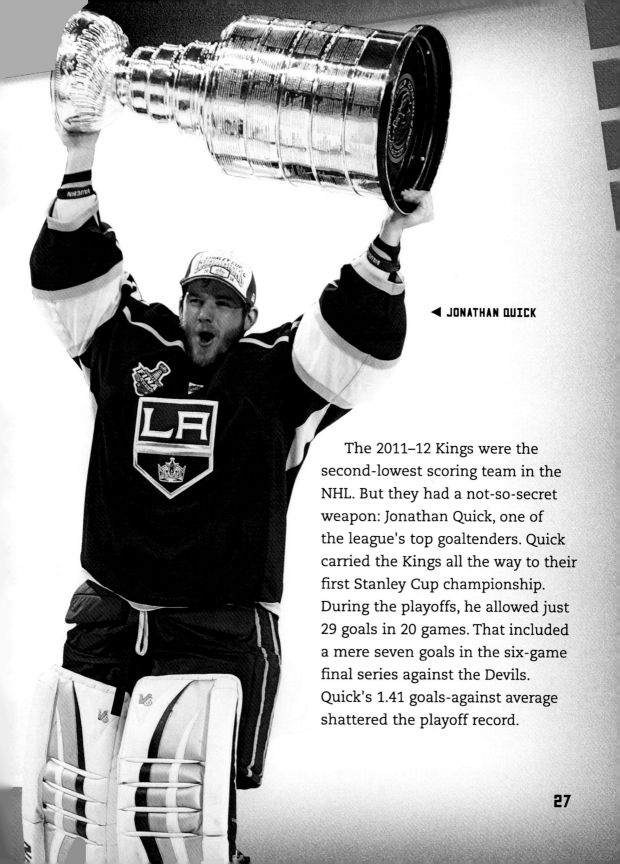

◀ JONATHAN QUICK

The 2011–12 Kings were the second-lowest scoring team in the NHL. But they had a not-so-secret weapon: Jonathan Quick, one of the league's top goaltenders. Quick carried the Kings all the way to their first Stanley Cup championship. During the playoffs, he allowed just 29 goals in 20 games. That included a mere seven goals in the six-game final series against the Devils. Quick's 1.41 goals-against average shattered the playoff record.

A CHANGED GAME

The best goals-against averages in NHL history belonged to the sport's earliest goaltenders. But those were in the days when only forward passing was allowed inside the offensive zone, and there were fewer scoring chances. Hockey evolved to create more scoring chances, with backward passing legalized in 1929–30 and, later, the two-line pass rule eliminated. The Montreal Canadiens' George Hainsworth is the only goalie to allow less than one goal per game in a season, with a 0.92 GAA in 1928–29. Alec Connell, who played from 1924 to 1937, owns the career record at 1.91.

▶ GEORGE HAINSWORTH

BEST SINGLE-SEASON GAA, 2005 TO 2015

Rank	Player	Team	Goals	Season
1.	JONATHAN QUICK	KINGS	1.95	2011–12
2.	CAREY PRICE	CANADIENS	1.96	2014–15
3.	HENRIK LUNDQVIST	RANGERS	1.97	2011–12
4.	MIIKKA KIPRUSOFF	FLAMES	2.07	2005–06
5.	PEKKA RINNE	PREDATORS	2.12	2010–11

Even though games are won and lost by teams, goaltenders are credited with wins and losses as well. Martin Brodeur set the record for most wins in a season with 48 in 2006–07. That same year, Roberto Luongo of the Vancouver Canucks won 47 games, which would have tied the previous mark set by the Philadelphia Flyers' Bernie Parent in 1973–74. Gary Smith of the 1970–71 California Golden Seals had the most losses in a season with 48.

▲ CAREY PRICE

CHAPTER 7
SAVE PERCENTAGE

Many people in hockey believe save percentage is a more useful stat than GAA for measuring a goaltender's success. Save percentage is calculated by dividing the number of saves by total shots on goal. Most NHL goaltenders have save percentages above .910—or 91 percent.

Shots on goal are the number of goals plus shots saved by the goaltender. Shots that are off-target are counted as attempted shots. Those chances include shots fired high and wide, ones that clank off goal posts or crossbars, and others blocked by defensive players. Stat crews observing games from the press box keep track of all shots and determine whether pucks were on goal.

Save percentage isn't a perfect stat, however, because it includes all shots on goal—no matter how they get to the goaltender. By digging deeper, fans can examine how many shots come during even-strength situations and how many come during opponents' power plays. They can also look at the quality of shots. How many tough saves were made against breakaways, odd-man rushes, and shots from close in front of the goal? How many were easier saves on shots from the boards or the blue line?

▲ HENRIK LUNDQVIST

BEST SAVE PERCENTAGE
single season, 2005 to 2015

Rank	Player	Team	Save %	Season
1.	CAREY PRICE	CANADIENS	.933	2014–15
2.	MIKE SMITH	COYOTES	.930	2011–12
	HENRIK LUNDQVIST	RANGERS	.930	2011–12
	PEKKA RINNE	PREDATORS	.930	2010–11
5.	JONATHAN QUICK	KINGS	.929	2011–12

GOALIES WITH HART

Goaltenders don't win the Hart Trophy as the NHL's most valuable player very often, but when they do it's because they had a very special season. In 2014–15, the Montreal Canadiens' Carey Price became just the seventh goaltender to capture the award as the season's best player. Price carried his team into the playoffs with the best save percentage in the league, at .933. That means he stopped 93.3 percent of the shots he faced. Price saw a lot of shots that season: 1,953. Only four other goaltenders faced more. He stopped 1,823 of them and won 44 regular-season games.

► DOMINIK HASEK

One of the most acrobatic goaltenders ever to play in the NHL, Dominik Hasek played for four teams over 16 seasons. He won two Stanley Cups with the Detroit Red Wings. Hasek holds the record for career save percentage at .922. Described as having a Slinky for a spine and known for never giving up on a puck, he won the Hart Trophy twice while playing for the Buffalo Sabres.

PUTTING UP ZEROES

During the early days of the NHL, Alec Connell of the Ottawa Senators strung together six consecutive shutouts and didn't allow a goal in a span of 461 minutes, 29 seconds of play. The modern-era (post-1944) shutout-streak record belongs to the Phoenix Coyotes' Brian Boucher. In 2004 he shut out five opponents in a row and went 332 minutes, 1 second between goals allowed. Boucher made 146 saves in his streak, which broke the modern record, set in 1949.

▶ BOBBY ORR

In the 1950s, the Montreal Canadiens tried to measure the impact individual skaters had on the game. The Canadiens counted the number of goals scored for and against the team while each player was on the ice. It was the birth of the plus-minus stat. The NHL began tracking it for all players a decade later.

A player receives a plus if he's on the ice when his team scores a goal. He receives a minus if he's on the ice when the opponent scores a goal. The only exceptions are for power-play goals. No plus or minus is tallied in those cases. However, there are pluses and minuses for short-handed goals.

Plus-minus provides a simple look at the brilliance of superstar Bobby Orr. Skating for the Boston Bruins, Orr changed the way defensemen played hockey. He didn't sit back on the blue line when his team had the puck. He jumped in the rush, carried the puck deep into the offensive zone, took shots, and scored goals. During the 1970–71 season, Orr won his second of three consecutive Hart Trophies as MVP. He had 139 points that season, a number that has never been eclipsed by another defenseman. Perhaps more impressive was his plus-minus. Orr was plus-124, still a record.

The Canadiens' Larry Robinson owns the career record for plus-minus. He was plus-730 for his 20-year career.

AN OUTDATED STAT?

Plus-minus has fallen out of favor with many of the game's followers. The NHL even stopped crowning a plus-minus champion in 2008. Critics say it's too broad and doesn't take into account several factors, including just how involved a player was in his team's scoring or giving up a goal.

The stat doesn't weigh the skills of the player's teammates, the ability of the goaltender, or the quality and number of shots generated or allowed. It's not considered a fair measurement for a "stay-at-home" defenseman who plays a lot of minutes or for a checking-line forward who specializes in defensive-zone faceoffs and coverage.

BEST +/- IN 2014-15 SEASON

Rank	Player	Team	+/-
1.	MAX PACIORETTY	CANADIENS	+38
	NIKITA KUCHEROV	LIGHTNING	+38
3.	TYLER JOHNSON	LIGHTNING	+33
4.	ONDREJ PALAT	LIGHTNING	+31
5.	JONATHAN TOEWS	BLACKHAWKS	+30

▲ MAX PACIORETTY

WORST +/- IN 2014-15 SEASON

Rank	Player	Team	+/-
1.	NAIL YAKUPOV	OILERS	-35
2.	TYLER BOZAK	MAPLE LEAFS	-34
	PHIL KESSEL	MAPLE LEAFS	-34
4.	TEDDY PURCELL	OILERS	-33
	JAMES VAN RIEMSDYK	MAPLE LEAFS	-33

In 2013–14, three-time Hart Trophy winner Alex Ovechkin led the NHL with 51 goals. However, he was a shocking minus-35 that season. Did that mean he was an unreliable defensive player? Should his coach have benched him? Of course not. Ovechkin was simply too important of a scoring threat to cut down his minutes. Still, he vowed to improve his plus-minus the next season and did, scoring 53 goals and finishing plus-10.

Tom Bladon of the Philadelphia Flyers was plus-10 during a single game in 1977. He had a big impact in the 11–1 win, too, scoring four goals and dishing out four assists. His eight points that night remain tied for the highest-scoring game ever by a defenseman.

CHAPTER 9

PUCK POSSESSION

▶ DREW DOUGHTY

In 2015 the NHL adopted some new ways of measuring players' and teams' performances—enhanced statistics that had been developed by other hockey observers. The stats originally had odd names, such as Corsi and Fenwick. Those are the names of the people who invented the stats. Considered more reliable than the plus-minus, they track puck possession. Teams usually win more games when they spend more time in control of the puck than their opponents. Successful teams tend to have the puck more during even-strength situations. They tend to spend more time playing in their offensive zone. They also take shots and get them on net.

The Corsi stat measures all attempted shots for and against a team or for and against a player while he's on the ice. The stat is also called shots attempted (or SAT), and it includes blocked shots. The stat was named after

▶ JIM CORSI

Jim Corsi, a former NHL player who became a goaltending coach. He came up with the number. He was trying to figure out how much work a goaltender had to do as he reacted to every shot. He soon found the numbers he gathered also showed how much time a player or team spent attacking versus defending.

Here's how you figure out a player's Corsi number: Add up his team's total shots attempted while he was on the ice; then subtract the total number of shots allowed. In the 2014–15 season, Kings defenseman Drew Doughty had the best Corsi number, plus-410.

CREDIT THE DEFENSE

The Fenwick number is also called unblocked shots attempted (or USAT). It is similar to Corsi except it does not include blocked shots. That's because blocked shots are considered skilled defensive plays that shouldn't count against a team or player. It was named after Matt Fenwick, a blogger who covered the Calgary Flames. Drew Doughty also had the best Fenwick in the 2014–15 season, at plus-285.

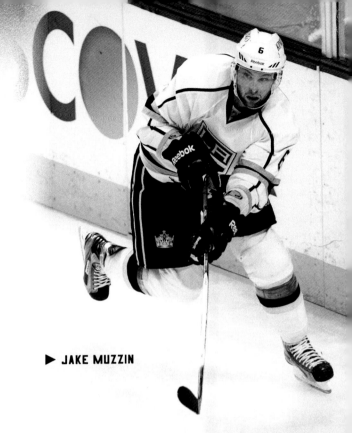

▶ JAKE MUZZIN

BEST CORSI, 2014–15 SEASON

Rank	Player	Team	Corsi
1.	DREW DOUGHTY	KINGS	+410
2.	JAKE MUZZIN	KINGS	+401
3.	ANZE KOPITAR	KINGS	+363
4.	JOE THORNTON	SHARKS	+353
5.	MIKE RIBEIRO	PREDATORS	+343

BEST FENWICK, 2014-15 SEASON

Rank	Player	Team	Fenwick
1.	DREW DOUGHTY	KINGS	+285
2.	JAKE MUZZIN	KINGS	+277
3.	NICK LEDDY	ISLANDERS	+264
4.	ANZE KOPITAR	KINGS	+263
5.	JOE THORNTON	SHARKS	+262

▲ DREW DOUGHTY

Corsi and Fenwick numbers can be broken down into several categories. They can measure how effective players are when their team is ahead, behind, or tied. Statisticians also measure them in close games. That includes one-goal or tied games in the first or second period, or tied games in the third period. During those times, teams are not changing their style of play to add offense or protect leads.

SHOT-BLOCKER SUPREME

Calgary Flames defenseman Kris Russell might be the bravest or foolhardiest player in the NHL. In 2014–15 he led the league in blocked shots. Without the benefit of goalie gear, he helped out his goalies by flinging his body in front of 283 shots that season, an NHL record.

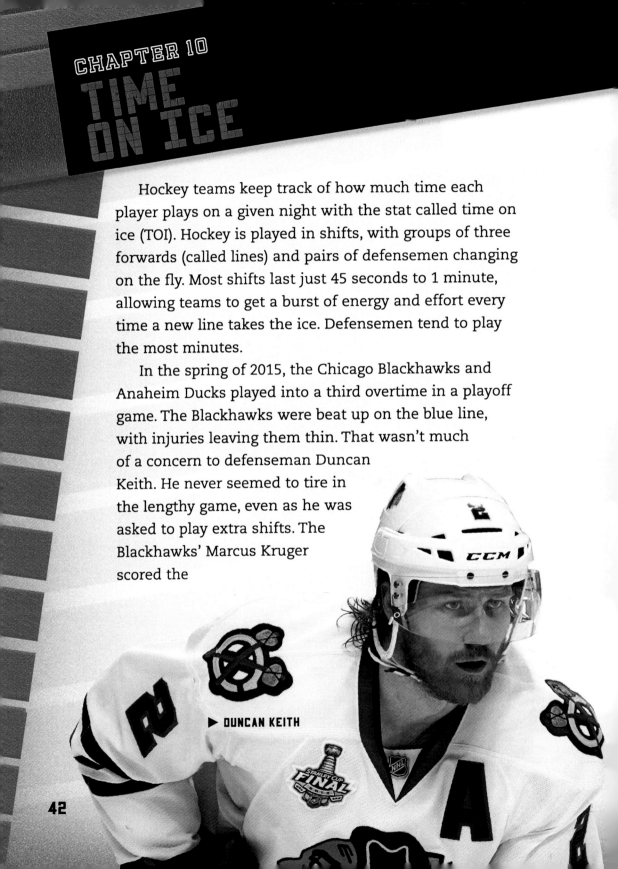

CHAPTER 10

TIME ON ICE

Hockey teams keep track of how much time each player plays on a given night with the stat called time on ice (TOI). Hockey is played in shifts, with groups of three forwards (called lines) and pairs of defensemen changing on the fly. Most shifts last just 45 seconds to 1 minute, allowing teams to get a burst of energy and effort every time a new line takes the ice. Defensemen tend to play the most minutes.

In the spring of 2015, the Chicago Blackhawks and Anaheim Ducks played into a third overtime in a playoff game. The Blackhawks were beat up on the blue line, with injuries leaving them thin. That wasn't much of a concern to defenseman Duncan Keith. He never seemed to tire in the lengthy game, even as he was asked to play extra shifts. The Blackhawks' Marcus Kruger scored the

▶ DUNCAN KEITH

game-winning goal with less than four minutes remaining in the third overtime. That's nearly an entire extra game after the third period had ended in a tie. By the end, Keith had been on the ice for 49 minutes, 51 seconds.

For each game, a stat crew in the press box keeps track of time on ice. They use a software program and mark when players go on and off the ice for line changes. Fans can even monitor a player's time on ice (and other stats) in real time online.

2014-15 TIME ON ICE LEADERS (AVERAGE PER GAME)

Rank	Player	Team	Time on Ice
1.	RYAN SUTER	WILD	29:03
2.	DREW DOUGHTY	KINGS	28:59
3.	ERIK KARLSSON	SENATORS	27:15
4.	ROMAN JOSI	PREDATORS	26:28
5.	SHEA WEBER	PREDATORS	26:22

 ▶ RYAN SUTER

STAT STARS

MOST POINTS IN A GAME

On February 7, 1976, Toronto Maple Leafs center Darryl Sittler scored six goals and had four assists for a 10-point game.

MOST GOALS IN A GAME

Joe Malone of the Quebec Bulldogs scored seven goals in one night in 1920.

▲ JOE MALONE

HIGHEST SAVE PERCENTAGE, SEASON

In 2012–13 the Ottawa Senators' Craig Anderson had a save percentage of .941.

MOST PENALTY MINUTES, CAREER

Tiger Williams racked up 3,966 minutes in penalties over 14 seasons with five teams.

CONSECUTIVE PENALTY KILLS

In 1999–2000 the Washington Capitals killed off 53 consecutive power plays.

MOST GOALTENDER WINS, CAREER

Martin Brodeur won 691 games in his 22-year career. All but three of those wins came with the New Jersey Devils.

▲ MARTIN BRODEUR

MOST GAMES PLAYED, CAREER

Gordie Howe played in 1,767 NHL games. He also played in 419 World Hockey Association games and retired from the NHL when he was 51 years old.

MOST CHAMPIONSHIPS WON BY A SINGLE PLAYER

Henri Richard of the Montreal Canadiens won 11 Stanley Cups.

MOST POWER PLAY GOALS, CAREER

Dave Andreychuk scored 274 times with the man advantage, playing for six teams between 1982 and 2006.

MOST SHORT-HANDED GOALS IN A SINGLE GAME

Theoren Fleury of the Calgary Flames scored three shorties while killing penalties one night in 1991.

MOST HAT TRICKS, CAREER

Wayne Gretzky had 50 hat tricks while playing for the Oilers, Kings, Blues, and Rangers.

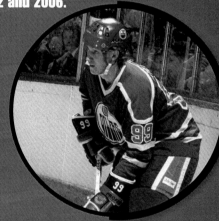

▲ WAYNE GRETZKY

CONSECUTIVE GAMES PLAYED BY A GOALIE

Glenn Hall played in 502 straight games—551 with playoff games included—from 1955 to 1962.

MOST SAVES IN A REGULATION GAME

Sam LoPresti of the Chicago Blackhawks stopped 80 of 83 shots in a loss to the Boston Bruins in a game in 1941.

STAT GLOSSARY

assist—a pass or touch of the puck that sets up a goal; up to two assists can be awarded on any goal

Corsi—also called shots attempted (SAT), this stat shows the difference between the number of attempted shots for and attempted shots against (including blocked shots) a team or a specific player when he's on the ice during even-strength situations

faceoff percentage—the percentage of faceoffs a player wins; equals wins divided by total faceoffs

Fenwick—also called unblocked shots attempted (USAT), this is the difference between the number of attempted shots for and attempted shots against (excluding blocked shots) a team or a specific player when he's on the ice during even-strength situations

game-winning goal—the goal that gave the winning team one more goal than the losing team

goals-against average (GAA)—The average number of goals allowed by a goaltender over a 60-minute time span

penalties in minutes (PIM)—a measurement of a player's penalties by counting the minutes assigned to each penalty (2 for a minor, 5 for a major, 10 for any misconduct or match penalty)

penalty kill percentage—the success rate of a team's penalty kill; divide successful kills by opponents' power plays

plus-minus (+/-)—the number of goals scored for a team minus the number scored against a team while a certain player is on the ice

point—any goal or assist

power play percentage (PP%)—the success rate of a team's power play; found by dividing the number of times a team scores with the man advantage by the total number of power play opportunities

save percentage (SV%)—the percentage of pucks stopped by a goaltender; found by dividing a goalie's save total by the number of shots on goal he faced

shot on goal—any shot at the goal that is either stopped by the goaltender or goes in for a goal; blocked shots and shots off the pipe that surrounds the net do not count

time on ice (TOI)—the total number of minutes a player plays in the game

READ MORE

Doeden, Matt. *Sidney Crosby: Hockey Superstar.* Sports Illustrated Kids: Superstar Athletes. North Mankato, Minn.: Capstone Press, 2012.

Frederick, Shane. *The Ultimate Collection of Pro Hockey Records.* Sports Illustrated Kids: For the Record. North Mankato, Minn: Capstone Press, 2013.

Jordan, Christopher. *We Are the Goal Scorers: The Top Point Leaders of the NHL.* New York: Fenn/Tundra, 2013.

INTERNET SITES

FactHound offers a safe, fun way to find Internet sites related to this book. All of the sites on FactHound have been researched by our staff.

Here's all you do:

Visit *www.facthound.com*

Type in this code: 9781491482179

 Check out projects, games and lots more at
www.capstonekids.com

INDEX